GLASS HOUSE OF DREAMS

"*My garden of flowers is also my garden of thoughts and dreams. The thoughts grow as freely as the flowers, and the dreams are as beautiful.*"

— Abram L. Urban

Published by Palm House Studios, Inc.
11350 McCormick Road, E.P.1, Suite 502
Hunt Valley, Maryland 21031
www.palmhousestudios.com

Text © 2010 Margaret Haviland Stansbury
Photographs © 2010 David Simpson Imagery
Design by Paula A. Simon, Highmeadow Design
All historic postcards are from the collection
of the author.

Printed at Everbest Printing Company, Nansha,
China through Four Colour Print Group,
Louisville, Kentucky
June 7, 2010   EPC-RN-95027

ISBN 978-0-9828704-0-2

MARGARET HAVILAND STANSBURY

Margaret "Peggy" Stansbury

GLASS HOUSE OF DREAMS

BALTIMORE'S VICTORIAN GLASS PALACE IN THE PARK

PHOTOGRAPHS BY DAVID SIMPSON

PALM HOUSE STUDIOS, INC.   MARYLAND

DEDICATION

"Foster the traditions of America that those who follow may benefit from the example of those who went before."
— PHILLIP DANA ORCUTT

THIS BOOK IS DEDICATED TO THE HONORABLE HOWARD PETERS RAWLINGS, a brilliant statesmen who believed in his city and the power of education. The glass house in Druid Hill Park, previously known as The Baltimore Conservatory, was renamed the Howard Peters Rawlings Conservatory and Botanical Gardens in his honor.

FOREWORD

BALTIMORE HAS LONG BEEN A LABORATORY FOR URBAN PLANNING IN AMERICA. From its early foray in the "City Beautiful Movement" in the late 1800's to the well known transformation of the Inner Harbor from an industrial center to an "Urban Entertainment Center" a century later, Baltimore has borrowed from the best of planning theories and put into practice models for the nation.

The creation of Druid Hill Park and the Conservatory that calls it home is a studied example of a design approach used to create social change in the city. The Conservatory is not only a beautiful example of Victorian architecture, it fulfils a goal to bring culture and natural life to the urban center.

Baltimore has long been known as the "City of Monuments" because of buildings like this one. As one of the few glass palaces remaining in America, it is an example of an architectural style and social philosophy that deserves commemoration.

This book by Margaret Haviland Stansbury demonstrates a loving commitment to not only the preservation of this delicate structure and its gardens, but to the ideals that led to its establishment in 1888 during the early years of the urban park movement. Her tenacious research and advocacy for the preservation and restoration of this important civic building have given future generations a great treasure. David Simpson's artful photography beautifully illustrates the Conservatory and the wonders of nature it houses.

We owe a debt of gratitude to those who worked so hard over the last decade to preserve the Conservatory and ensure its longevity as an architectural masterpiece and an educational center for city dwellers. Lovers of gardens, devotees of history, architectural enthusiasts and even students of civil rights will find much to appreciate in the publication of this beautiful photographic essay that follows the evolution of the Baltimore Conservatory to the Howard Peters Rawlings Conservatory and Botanical Gardens.

— JANET MARIE SMITH
Vice President of Planning and Development
for the Baltimore Orioles

CONSERVATORY AT ROSE GARDENS, DRUID HILL PARK, BALTIMORE, MD.

3A-H196

UNITED
STATES
POSTAGE

1 CENT 1

Dear Violet

We reached here this
at 4 o'clock standard
time, had supper &
went bowling. Yesterday
we went to see
Lock Raven & it was
beautiful. Tonight we
are going skating at
Carlins. We are having
the greatest time but
the weather is so warm!
Your friend Elizabeth

Miss Violet Matthews
109 King St.
East Bristol,
Conn.

PREFACE

IN 2009, DAVID SIMPSON RELEASED A BOOK OF PHOTOGRAPHY TITLED *LOCH RAVEN* about a local reservoir of the same name. This vast body of water has not only quenched thirsts but also provides a natural setting for the citizens of Baltimore City and its surrounding areas. The forest, waters and open land allow for a myriad of outdoor activities. David has spent countless hours in Loch Raven, from kayaking to teaching his children how to ride a bicycle. Using his skill as a cinematographer and fine arts photographer, he set out to document and highlight this local gem. His efforts culminated in a stunning and immensely enjoyable book.

I fell in love with *Loch Raven* and purchased copies for family and friends. The book was not only visually entertaining but also brought back my own childhood memories of the reservoir. After discovering the book, I was pleasantly surprised to learn that David Simpson was scheduled to speak at the Rotary Club of Hunt Valley, Maryland. I shared with my fellow Rotarians how wonderful it was that David had captured such a treasure in our own back yard. After his lecture, I had a chance to meet David and shared with him my own story of local preservation. As a former student and teacher at the Maryland Institute College of Art, David was very familiar with the 1888 glass house sitting in Druid Hill Park. He encouraged me to write a book and commemorate the spirit of the Baltimore Conservatory, a place that holds my heart, as he did with Loch Raven. Although we were strangers to each other, in a very brief period of time we decided to combine our efforts to create a book that would preserve the history of the Conservatory, which, like Loch Raven, is a place of extraordinary beauty. It is a place for people to share collectively, to come together in mutual appreciation for nature. They are both remarkable Baltimore landmarks and deserve to be recorded for a wide audience to enjoy.

To help capture the Conservatory's past, I have researched and collected beautiful antique postcards featuring this architectural gem. These postcards date from the late 1800's to the mid 20th century, and are a great way to see the conservatory's appearance at these times. One of the very first cards acquired for the project features an image of the original Palm House. The postcard was mailed from Baltimore to Connecticut in 1940. Carefully preserved by a collector in Arizona, the handwritten note features an account of the sender's trip to Baltimore, including her trip to see Loch Raven, writing, "Yesterday we went to see Loch Raven and it was beautiful. We are having the greatest time." This postcard and its contents were a clear sign to me that my dream of a book was meant to become a reality.

— MARGARET HAVILAND STANSBURY

DRIVE AND CONSERVATORY—DRUID HILL PARK, BALTIMORE, MD.

Hand-Colored.

GLASS HOUSE OF DREAMS: AN INTRODUCTION

"Flowers seem intended for the solace of ordinary humanity."
— JOHN RUSKIN

MANY ARE FASCINATED WITH GLASS HOUSES, from kings and queens to the common man. The lush smells and bright colors of the exotic plants enclosed in these buildings are at once striking and transformational. Early greenhouses were utilitarian, built to protect plants during cold winters. But these structures evolved to become the focal points of gardens. With the advent of the mass production of iron, steel, and large sheets of glass, the rudimentary greenhouses became architectural wonders. Glass houses became the rage of the mid 19th century, beginning in England and spreading throughout Europe due to World Fairs and exhibitions. Two conservatories built in England caused much fanfare. The 1848 Palm House at the Royal Botanic Gardens at Kew, designed by Richard Turner and Decimus Burton, quickly became one of the most popular destinations in England. Landscape gardener Joseph Paxton amazed the world with his winning design for the colossal Crystal Palace in London's Great Exhibition of 1857.

Glass house fever was soon caught in America when the first glass conservatory was constructed at the New York World's Fair in 1853. Philadelphia also built a glass house, named Horticultural Hall, in Fairmount Park for the Philadelphia Centennial Exposition of 1876. Sadly, both of these early structures were destroyed by fire. But this was only the beginning for glass houses in America. During the same time of interest in this new architectural phenomenon, there was a large movement for the development of parks in the urban centers of the nation. This concept was also transported from Europe, which had already begun creating sanctuaries from urban industrial life. The first of these parks in America, Central Park in New York, was designed by Frederick Law Olmsted and Calvert Vaux in 1858. This first park strongly influenced the development of others like it

Conservatory, Druid Hill Park, Baltim

12195

2

throughout the country. Conservatories were an important part of this new landscape. The glass house became a gathering place to soothe tired citizens and entertain them with exotic plants from around the world.

Baltimore's dream of a glass house would begin under Mayor Thomas Swann. Mayor Swann appointed John H. B. Latrobe to head the Baltimore City Parks Commission and to locate an area of land to create a park for the city. The planners decided on Druid Hill, an exquisite property in the Rogers/Buchanan family estate. The land had been nurtured with a keen horticultural eye and was a perfect choice. The city of Baltimore purchased the lands in 1860 and set out to turn it into a public space. Howard Daniels, an engineer and landscape designer, was hired to create walls, drives and lakes for the future park. Daniels, a contemporary of Frederick Law Olmsted, traveled throughout England and Europe to study parks and English landscape gardening. The commission also hired a young architect, 19-year-old George Aloysius Frederick, to create buildings and pavilions (including a glass house) to enhance the landscape of open lawns, groves and woodlands. A plot of land was selected and retained for the building of a conservatory in 1873, but due to financial limitations actual construction didn't begin until 1887.

In 1888, arguably the second oldest surviving glass house in America was completed in Baltimore's Druid Hill Park. The Victorian-style glass house was built with an impressive 175 windows, and possessed a soaring ninety foot roof. An orchid room was also built along with the rest of the structure. Baltimore now had a world class conservatory to call its own.

During the mid-19th century, Parks Commissioner Howard Latrobe and Parks Designer Howard Daniels embarked on their own grand tours of Europe. Daniels and Latrobe could have very possibly encountered the stunning Vienna Palmhaus, built in 1873 for the Vienna World's Exhibition. Upon observation, striking similarities can be seen between the Palmhaus and Baltimore's Conservatory. Daniels and Latrobe may very well have influenced the young architect George Frederick on his design of a glass house for Baltimore.

Madison Avenue Gate Druid Hill Park, Baltimore, Md.

Scene Along the Shor

Baltimore, Md Band Stand, Druid Hill Park.

Winter Scene in Druid Hill Park, Baltimore, Md.

Scene on the Lake, Druid Hill Park, Baltimore Md.

9352. Mansion House & Flock of sheep, Baltimore, Md.

G 418a. The Conservatory, Druid-

Accept-ta-so in

...servoir Druid Hill Park, Baltimore, Md.

...ltimore, Md.

Conservatory. Patterson Park.   BALTIMORE, MD.

Baltimore City originally built four splendid glass houses in Carroll Park, Clifton Park, Druid Hill Park and Patterson Park. The Great Depression and austerity of the war years greatly impacted funding for these beautiful structures. Suffering from lack of maintenance, all but the Druid Hill Park structure sadly were demolished. The Baltimore Conservatory survived these difficult times and was preserved by a group of dedicated citizens and city workers.

Lawn Tennis Grounds and Conservatory, Druid Hill Park. BALTIMORE, Md.

HAND-COLORED.

The Conservatory and Tennis Courts,
Druid Hill Park, Baltimore, Md.

DREAMS OF EQUALITY

Many citizens of Baltimore have fond memories of the clay tennis courts located beside the Conservatory. These courts were not only a source of athletic enjoyment, but also the setting for American civil rights history. In July of 1948, the Progressive Party of Maryland staged an interracial tennis match on the segregated courts in protest of the racist rules in place. Police stopped the match, and seven people were charged with conspiracy to disturb the peace. They appealed their case to the Supreme Court, but were denied a review of the case. This protest was instrumental in the desegregation of all Baltimore public recreational facilities six years later, and was a cause of hope for a bright future of diversity and understanding in Baltimore City.

DREAMS OF PRESERVATION AND EDUCATION

Over one hundred years after the Baltimore Park Board built the Conservatory a non-profit organization was formed to act as stewards for this local treasure. The Baltimore Conservatory Association was created in 1997, with a mission to restore the original Palm House and expand the existing facilities. The goal was to create a living museum for educational purposes. The Association worked in partnership with the city of Baltimore to design an expanded facility, as well as to raise the funds needed to make this plan a reality. The 1888 Palm House and Orchid Room were restored to their former glory, and two smaller buildings were added to accommodate additional visitors. These buildings were also intended to hold wedding receptions and other events. The three connecting greenhouses were revitalized with displays of plant life from around the world. Now a visit to the Conservatory can take one through the Mediterranean, a desert, and a tropical paradise all in one trip. The Conservatory has been transformed into a living classroom for teaching environmental, social and cultural lessons. Not only is this beautiful structure a place for rare plants, it has also made a positive impact on children, opening their eyes to the world around them.

1854—The Golden Gate Park Conservatory, San Francisco, California.

SAN FRANCISCO'S GLASS HOUSE
Built in 1879, San Francisco's Conservatory of Flowers is the oldest surviving municipal wood and glass house in the United States.

THE LINNEAN HOUSE IN MISSOURI
The Linnean House of the Missouri Botanical Gardens is widely considered to be the second oldest surviving conservatory in the United States. The structure was designed in the Victorian tradition as an "orangerie," a building used to house citrus trees and other tropical plants over winter. The roof was constructed with half slate and half glass materials. The building also possesses a Georgian design and Palladian windows. Due to these design elements and materials, it can be argued that Baltimore's Conservatory is truly the second oldest glass house in the United States.

"Can we conceive what humanity would be if it did not know the flowers?"
— MAURICE MAETERLINCK

32

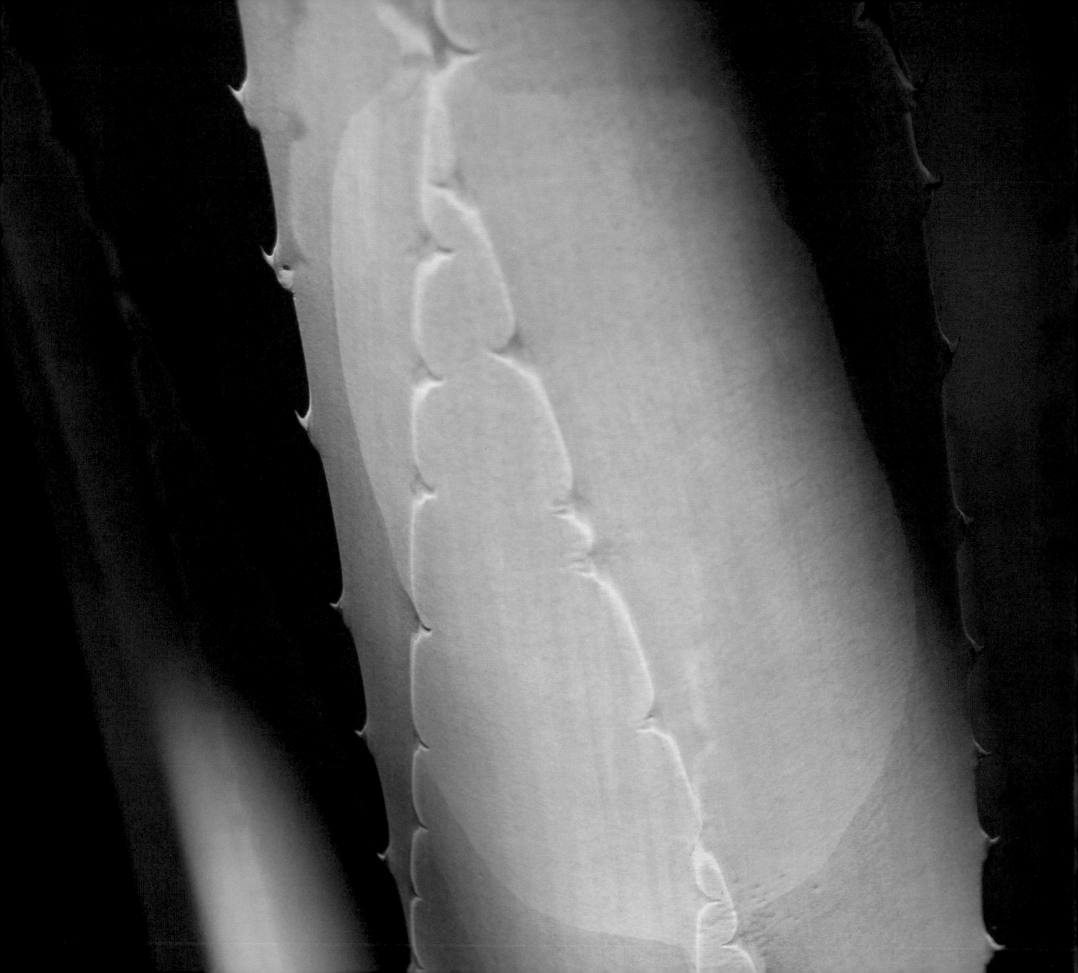

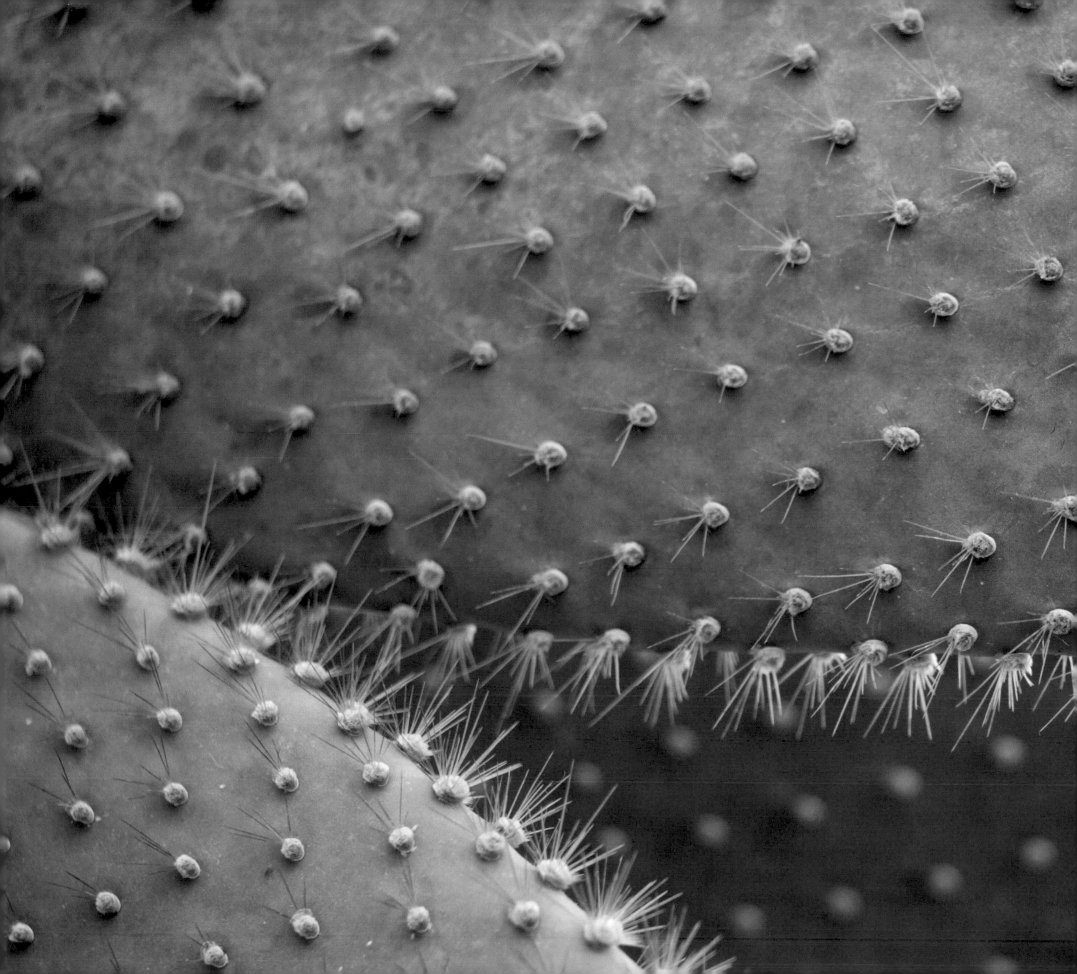

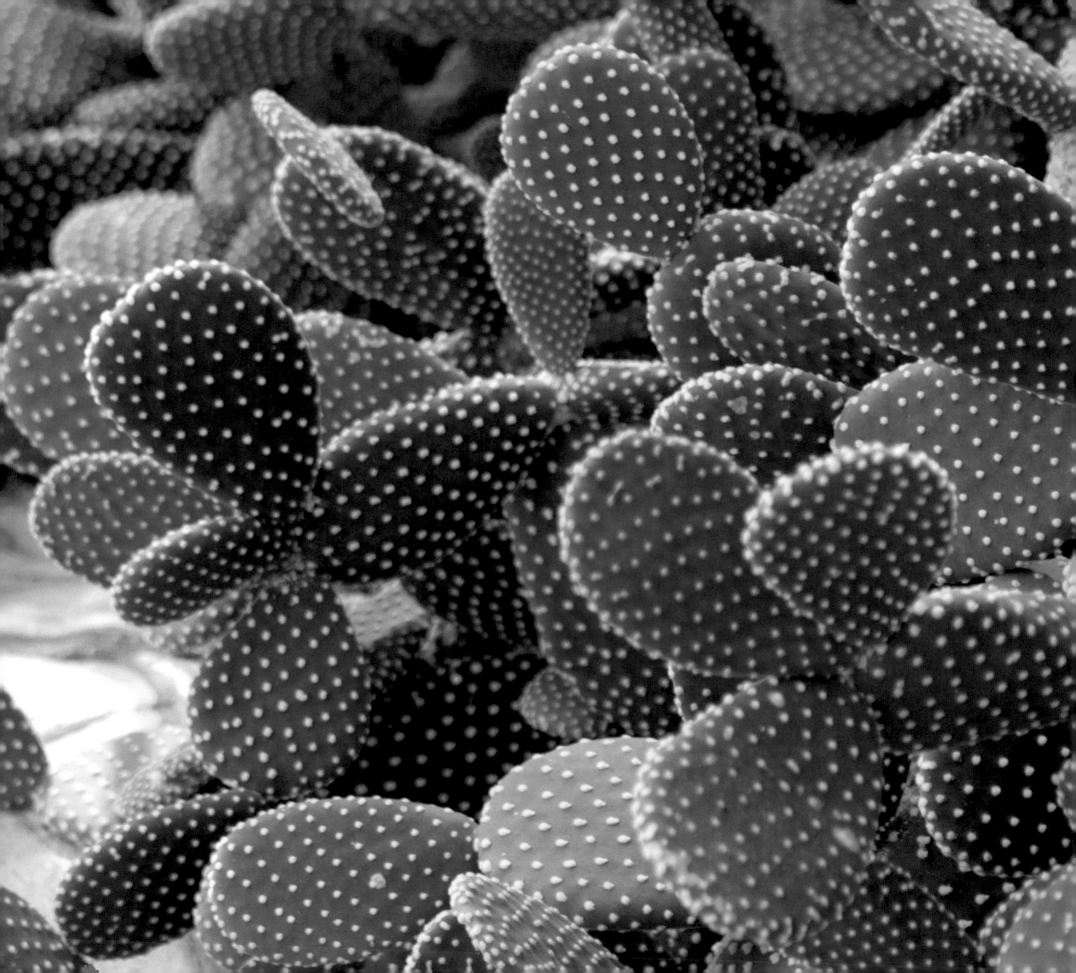

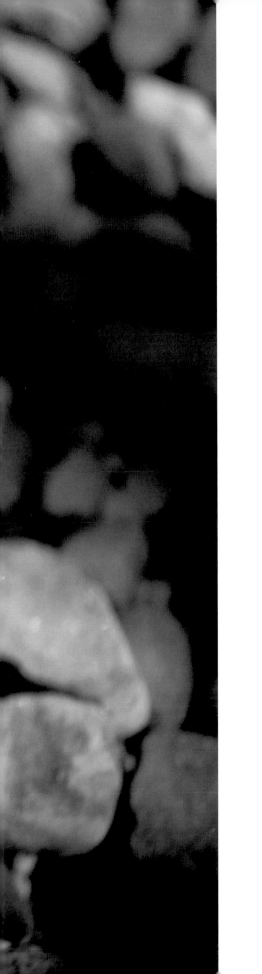

ACKNOWLEDGEMENTS

I would like to recognize and thank the individuals who volunteered their time and talents as stewards of the Howard Peters Rawlings Conservatory and Botanic Gardens.

BALTIMORE CONSERVATORY ASSOCIATION (BCA) FOUNDING BOARD MEMBERS:

Jane Baldwin, Mark Cameron, Dennis Fiori,
Barbara Gumbinger Bien, Anne O. Emery,
Ellie Heldrich, JoAnn Hitt, Edith Howard-Henry,
Greta Jackson, Anne Madden, Bridget Maginn,
John Pumphrey, John Sanders, Elizabeth Shively,
Paula A. Simon, Janet Marie Smith, Sandra R. Sparks,
Richard T. Stansbury, Barry Woolf

ADDITIONAL BCA BOARD MEMBERS:

Emily Alt, Marianne Armstrong, Delores F. Baden, Leigh Barnes,
Pat Cullen, Donna Cypress, Kelly Fitzgerald, Suzan Garabedian,
Kathryn Miller Goldman, Isodore Goodman, Marion Queensbury-Griner,
David Hart, Brian Haysbert, Fred Hiser, George Hill, Elizabeth Hopkins,
Lemuel (Arthur) Lewie, A. Lee Lundy, Jr., Diana Kane, Lolita Kelson,
The Honorable Sharon H. May, Dawn McCleary, Phyllis Meyers,
Carla Moose, Scott Rykiel, Sidney Silber, Emma Stokes,
Karen J. Stults, Douglas A. Williams

WITH SPECIAL THANKS TO:

The Federated Garden Clubs of Maryland, 4,000 members strong,
whose initial support in Annapolis and their continued support made
the revitalization of this Conservatory possible.

Mr. Michael J. Baker, for sharing his expertise in governmental relations.

Mr. David W. Hillery, CPA, for sharing his financial expertise with
our non-profit organization.

EARLY SUPPORTERS OF OUR EFFORT:

Timothy Almaguer, Roger Birkel, Elaine Born, Beverly C. Bridger, Michael R. Butler, Mary Ellen Didion, Regi Goldberg, Fredye Gross, Jean Hinman, Nancy Hopkins, Beth Hunter, Ellie Kelly, Hazel Kidd, Gay Legg, Paul W. Madden, Kim Meagher, George K. Mister, Elizabeth MacGlashan Nelson, Herbert R. Plitt, Karen Offutt, Jill Palkovitz, Patricia Pickett, Mae W. Scott, Ann Simmons, Dennis Simon, Carolyn Smith, Bonnie Stevens, Alma R. Turner, Betsy Wendell-Dugan, Yvonne West, Lissa Williamson, John I. Wilson, Brucie Wright

IN RECOGNITION OF THE DEDICATED EFFORTS
OF THE CITY OF BALTIMORE AND ITS EMPLOYEES:

Baltimore City Department of Recreation and Parks and the Baltimore City Department of Recreation and Parks Advisory Board

Baltimore City Department of Public Works

Horticulture Division of Baltimore City Department of Recreation and Parks: Bill Vondrasek, Kate Blom, Melissa Grim

TO THE DEDICATED AND KNOWLEDGEABLE STAFF
OF THE RAWLINGS CONSERVATORY:

Kate Blom, Conservatory and Greenhouse Supervisor; Sandy Reagan, Angela Archable, George Cannoles, Don Dorrm, Alice Hisley, Robert Horton, Sheila Johnson, Mark Johnson, Margie Jones, Carol Kalakay, Michael Lemmon, Betsy Nettelbeck, Beth Succop, Erin Sullivan and the volunteers whose efforts keep the Conservatory functional *and* beautiful.

RENOVATION DESIGN AND CONSTRUCTION FIRMS:

Landscapes LA • Planning • HP, Patricia O'Donnell, Principal
Kann & Associates, Roger Katzenberg, Project Architect
Southway Builders

THOSE WHO ASSISTED WITH THIS BOOK:

Book Design/Packaging, Paula A. Simon, Highmeadow Design
Assistant Editor, John Rignal Stansbury
Proofreading/Editing Services, Christianna McCausland

AND LAST BUT NOT LEAST:

A most sincere thank you to my husband Richard T. Stansbury, attorney extraordinaire, who gave his time, talent and treasure to the Conservatory.

A special thank you to my sons Jack Stansbury and Alex Stansbury, who spent many of their childhood days attending civic meetings at the Conservatory to make this dream come true.

LIST OF PLANTS

Page 10-11   Sago Palm, *Cycad (left)*; Christmas Palm, *Veitchia merrillii (right)*

Page 12   Bismark Palm - detail, *Bismarkia nobilis*

Page 13   Lady Palm, *Rhapis excelsa;* Coconut Palm, *Cocos nucifera;* Bismark Palm, *Bismarkia nobilis;* Palm Grass, *Curculigo capitulata*

Page 14   Cabada Palm - detail, *Chrysalidocarpus cabadae*

Page 16   Bismark Palm, *Bismarkia nobilis (left);* Foxtail Palm, *Wodyetia bifurcata (top right)*

Page 17   Pin-Stripe Plant, *Calathea Roseo-lineata*

Page 18   Torch Ginger, *Nicolaia elatior 'Thompsonae'*

Page 19   Fishtail Palm, *Caryota mitis*

Page 21   Dwarf Tree Fern, *Blechnum gibbum 'Silver Lady'*

Page 22   Orchid - Dancing Lady, *Oncidium sp.,* Protea

Page 26   Orchid, *Vanda ASDA John De Biase 'Angela'*

Page 28   Orchid, *Cattleya 'Hawaiin Wedding' HCC-AOS*

Page 29   Orchid, *Dendrobium Pink Surprise*
Orchid, *Brassocattleya Hybrid*

Page 33   Orchid, *Dendrobium Burana 'Pink Lady'*

Page 34   Orchid, *Brassavola Laelio Cattleya Hybrid*

Page 35   Paper Flower, *Bougainvillea glabra*

Page 36   Paper Flower, *Bougainvillea glabra*

Page 37   Hibiscus, *Hibiscus rosa-sinensis*

Page 39   Sunflowers, *Helianthus annuus*

Page 40   Queen Protea, *Protea neriifolia*

Page 41   Staghorn Fern, *Platycerium bifurcatum*

Page 42   Australian Tree Fern, *Cyathea cooperi (right)*; Purple Wreath, *Petrea volubilis (on arch)*; Brazilian Red Cloak, *Megaskepasma erythrochlamys (left)*

Page 43   Lobster Claw, *Heliconia bihai 'Island Yellow'*

Page 44   Tropical Fern, *Polypodium mandianum*

Page 45   Passion Flower, *Passiflora caerulea*

Page 46   Rangoon Creeper, *Quisqualis indica*

Page 47   Bromeliad, *Gusmania sp.*

Page 48-49   Banana - fruit and leaf detail, *Musa sp.*

Page 50   Bird of Paradise, *Strelitzia reginae*

Page 54   Water Lettuce, *Pistia stratiotes*

Page 56-57   Water Lilies

Page 58-59   Air Plant, *Tillandsia sp.*

Page 61   The Conservatory's mascot, Mango

Page 62   Century Plant - details, *Agave americana variegata*

Page 63   Century Plant, *Agave americana variegata (main);* Golden Barrel Cactus, *Echinocactus grusonii (foreground);* Blue Agave, *Agave americana (back left)*

Page 64-65   Blue Agave, *Agave americana*

Page 66   Century Plant, *Agave parvifola*

Page 67   Prickly Pear, *Opuntia microdasys 'Alba'*

Page 68   Coral Aloe, *Aloe striata*

Page 69   Echeveria - flower detail, *Echeveria sp.*

Page 70   Prickly Pear, *Opuntia microdasys 'Alba'*

Page 72   Cactus, *Stenocereus griseus*

Page 73   Sandstone boulder from the State of Utah

Page 74   Prickly Pear, *Opuntia dillenii*

Page 75   Tree Yucca, *Yucca filifera*

Page 76   Tree Aeonium, *Aeonium arboreum*

Page 77   Crown-of-Thorns, *Euphorbia milii var. splendens*

Page 78   Cactus, *Ferocactus sp.*; Cactus, *Stenocereus griseus*

Page 79   Madagascar Cactus, *Alluaudia procera*

Page 80   Skeleton of Saguaro Cactus, *Carnegiea gigantea*

Page 81   Elephant Ear - bulb, *Colocasia esculenta*

Page 85   Peony in watering can

Page 87   Iris on garden bench

ART AND OTHER PHOTOGRAPHY:

Page 3   The Palmhaus at Schonbrunn Palace in Vienna, Austria
          Photo © Jeff Whyte

Page 9   "In The Conservatory," oil painting on canvas by
          Édouard Manet, 1879

Page 20   Flower bouquet by Fleur de lis Florist, Baltimore, Md.

Page 31   Flower painting on glassware by Ann Holland Beeler
          (the author's grandmother)

Page 83   Entry plaza mosaic by renowned Baltimore artist
          Joyce J. Scott

Page 86   This unusual, multi-faceted sundial was created by Peter
          Hamilton and Waltersville Granite Quarry and given to
          the city of Baltimore around 1890.

All historic postcards are from the collection of the author.

BIBLIOGRAPHY:

Bowditch, Eden Unger, and Anne Draddy. *Druid Hill Park: The Heart of Historic Baltimore.* Charleston, SC: The History Press, 2008. Print.

Cunningham, Anne S. *Crystal Palaces: Garden Conservatories of the United States.* New York: Princeton Architectural, 2000. Print.

Kassinger, Ruth. *Paradise Under Glass: An Amateur Creates a Conservatory Garden.* New York, NY: William Morrow, 2010. Print.

Kohlmaier, Georg, and Barna Von. Sartory. *Houses of Glass: A Nineteenth-century Building Type.* Translated by John C. Harvey. Cambridge, Mass.: MIT, 1986. Print.

Sazevich, Nina. *Treasures of the Conservatory of Flowers.* Berkeley, Calif.: Heyday, 2006. Print.

Woods, May, and Arete Swartz Warren. *Glass Houses: A History of Greenhouses, Orangeries and Conservatories.* New York: Rizzoli, 1988. Print.

THE HOWARD PETERS RAWLINGS CONSERVATORY AND BOTANIC GARDENS
3100 Swan Drive in Druid Hill Park
Baltimore, Maryland 21217
(410) 396-0008
Open Tuesday - Sunday: 10 a.m. - 4 p.m.

"A flower's appeal is in its contradiction—delicate in form yet strong in fragrance, so small in size yet big in beauty, so short in life yet long on effect."
— Terri Guillemets